Living the Days of Lent 2013

edited by Ellen Dauwer, SC, and Mary Mc Cormick, SC

Paulist Press
New York / Mahwah, NJ

Cover design by Christina Cancel
Book design by Lynn Else

ISBN 978-0-8091-4746-5

Published by Paulist Press
997 Macarthur Boulevard
Mahwah, New Jersey 07430

www.paulistpress.com

Printed and bound in the
United States of America

Introduction

Once again we enter into the season of Lent, a time of prayer, fasting, and almsgiving. How do we begin this year? Is it with eager anticipation, foot-dragging reluctance, or something in between these extremes? What are our hopes for this holy season?

Instead of beginning with resolutions that might not last beyond the first week, it might be more helpful to begin by expressing our hopes. What are our hopes for our relationship with God in prayer? How and from what do we hope to fast? How do we hope to share both our surplus and our substance with the poor?

This collection of Lenten reflections is offered by the Sisters of Charity of New York and the Sisters of Charity of Saint Elizabeth of New Jersey. May the hopes and thoughts that they share inspire our days, sustain us as we enter into the Paschal Mystery, and challenge us as we journey to Easter.

Contributors
(in alphabetical order)

Sister Patricia Beaumont, SC
Sister Regina Bechtle, SC
Sister Sheila Brosnan, SC
Sister Mary Canavan, SC
Sister Anita Constance, SC
Sister Ellen Dauwer, SC
Sister Cheryl France, SC
Sister Barbara Garland, SC
Sister Vivienne Joyce, SC
Sister Eileen T. Kelly, SC
Sister Mary E. Mc Cormick, SC
Sister Noreen Neary, SC
Sister Margaret M. O'Brien, SC
Sister Ellen Rose O'Connell, SC
Sister Dominica Rocchio, SC
Sister Marilyn Thie, SC

Repent and Believe the Good News

"Ashes, ashes, we all fall down!"

I never understood that old nursery rhyme. But as I repeat it in the context of Ash Wednesday, it makes sense. We are signed with ashes as a reminder of how often we fall and need a time like Lent to help us to return to God with our whole heart.

Too often Lent reminds us of ashes, Stations of the Cross, even hot cross buns. Joel reminds us: external practices are good but not enough. He calls us to rend our hearts—to let God in to touch us—and invites us to return to him.

Lent is a time to make heartfelt efforts to return to a deep relationship with God. We then become good news not so much by what we do as by who we are: one with God and one another.

Today, "rend your hearts....
Return to the LORD, your God" (Joel 2:13).

Readings: Joel 2:12–18; Psalm 51; 2 Corinthians 5:20—6:2; Matthew 6:1–6, 16–18

Saving Through Loss

"For those who want to save their life will lose it, and those who lose their life for my sake will save it."
—Luke 9:24

A paradox: the more one loses one's life, the more one is enriched with life.

We all know loss: to lose some one or thing loved as precious is to lose part of ourselves.

There are several ways to lose one's life. The richest is to spend one's life for others, following Jesus as he lived before his death.

In Luke, we find a promise: to lose one's life by spending it for others, for justice's sake, is to find fuller, more meaningful life. Loss that occurs from generosity, giving of one's very self, is in effect to choose life.

This emphasis finds expression in Deuteronomy: "Choose life so that you and your descendants may live, loving the LORD your God" (Deut 30:19–20).

May we live the paradox that is Lent:
spending one's self for all is to gain renewed life.

Readings: Deuteronomy 30:15–20; Psalm 1; Luke 9:22–25

Fasting

*Then the disciples of John came to him, saying,
"why do we and the Pharisees fast often,
but your diciples do not fast?"*
—Matthew 9:14

Lenten practices of fasting *from* certain pleasures fall short of how today's readings invite us to fast. While refraining from something we like may be beneficial, it often leads us to focus more on the increased pleasure we'll enjoy once Lent is over.

This kind of Lenten practice of *giving up* something is, in effect, passive and negative. By contrast, today's readings call us to fast by doing, by acting in practical ways.

Confusion about fasting was alive in Jesus' time. He explained what God expected as fasting to those who wondered why Jesus' disciples did not fast as they did. What God calls for as fasting is most explicit in Isaiah 58:6–7:

> to loose the bonds of injustice,...
> to let the oppressed go free...
> to share your bread with the hungry,
> and bring the homeless poor into your house;
> when you see the naked, to cover them....

**Let us choose one of these directives to act on,
conscious that doing something positive to assist
another is the fasting God seeks.**

Readings: Isaiah 58:1–9a; Psalm 51; Matthew 9:14–15

The Still Point

"Follow me."
—Luke 5:27

Levi, the despised tax collector, and Jesus, the itinerant healer and preacher, glance at one another. In this visual encounter, their hearts are as one. Compunction and forgiveness spontaneously cement the newly formed relationship. Jesus points to the way and invites Matthew to "follow me" (Luke 5:27). Matthew swiftly leaves his controversial professional activity to step into the footprints of Jesus.

The table is set for the great celebration. Word goes out that sinners are the honored guests. Here comes everybody! Don't be left out!

Jesus wants to offer me love at a glance. Sometimes I want to shy away from that overture and focus instead on the behavior of others.

O God, help me this day to know your steadfast love. Give me an undivided heart and constancy of spirit so that I may follow you. When I am stressed, help me to be drawn to the still point, that moment in time when love embraces sorrow and forgiveness.

Readings: Isaiah 58:9b–14; Psalm 86; Luke 5:27–32

Letting Go

Jesus...was led by the Spirit in the wilderness....
—Luke 4:1

Where is the Spirit leading you this Lent? What wilderness might you find difficult to be in? Jesus was tempted by Satan to accumulate power, wealth, all his desires, if only he would deny God. Power can be *for* persons or *over* persons; it makes all the difference which way it is used. And power is often defined by wealth, by an overriding need to accumulate more, forgetting the needs of others. Our own controlling needs are caught up in desires beyond our reach.

What is the wilderness that you should enter this Lent? Is it letting go of control, or of the need to own more things? Perhaps it is a desire that interferes with another's fullness of life. Are these in keeping with the words of the Gospel?

Will you let the Spirit lead you to the wilderness this Lent, or will you need to direct the journey?

Readings: Deuteronomy 26:4–10; Psalm 91; Romans 10:8–13; Luke 4:1–13

Sifting and Sorting

"Just as you did it to one of the least of these who are members of my family, you did it to me."
—Matthew 25:40

Putting things in good order can be a very satisfying activity. Yet I find the vision of the last judgment at the throne of God quite unsettling. Jesus teaches his disciples that life is on a continuum with eternity.

Every day the media comes into my home and shows me the faces of people who are hungry, sick, naked, and imprisoned—and in need of human solace. I often feel helpless and paralyzed.

Lenten prayer, fasting, and almsgiving of time and resources offer the age-old antidote to my own comfort-seeking and neglect of God's family members. These disciplines help me to do something rather than be swallowed up in disregard or useless guilt.

Today, I pray to God for the courage and perseverance to sift and sort, hear and heed the call of Jesus during these Lenten days.

Readings: Leviticus 19:1–2, 11–18; Psalm 19; Matthew 25:31–46

Debt Forgiveness

*"And forgive us our debts, as we also
have forgiven our debtors."*
—Matthew 6:12

In our society, debt forgiveness is often a lengthy, complex process of political negotiation. By contrast, Jesus offers a simple formula to his disciples: Go to the Father. Present your need to be forgiven and your desire to forgive. Then pray to stay the course.

It is not necessary or helpful to try to bend God's will, for "...your Father knows what you need before you ask him" (Matt 6:8).

Debt relief happens when we draw down on the life of healing grace.

So shall my word be that goes out from my mouth;
it shall not return to me empty,
but it shall accomplish that which I purpose,
and succeed in the thing for which I sent it.
(Isa 55:11)

**During this Lenten season, I want to disengage from
ineffective soul searching. Procrastination and
self-righteousness will not deter me from approaching
the Father to ask for the grace of forgiveness
and the grace to forgive.**

Readings: Isaiah 55:10–11; Psalm 34; Matthew 6:7–15

Seeking Signs

"This generation...asks for a sign, but no sign will be given to it except the sign of Jonah."
—Luke 11:29

Signs are given to us in abundance. The sign of Jonah was a precursor of the resurrection. The crowds surrounding that astounding preacher, Jesus Christ, were always seeking a sign that what he said was real and true.

How often do we seek these signs! "God, if you grant my wish, then I will be a better father or mother...or I will lose twenty pounds...or I will...." Instead of living the life of redemption and resurrection, we bargain with God, don't we? Instead of simply trusting that God knows what is best for us, we want to tell God what that *best* is. The era we live in encourages self-reliance; God encourages reliance on him and trust in his outrageous goodness.

**Where do I most need to trust God today;
what *ifs* get in the way?**

Readings: Jonah 3:1–10; Psalm 51; Luke 11:29–32

Thursday, *February 21*

God's Loving Care

Though I walk in the midst of trouble...
you stretch out your hand,
and your right hand delivers me.

—Psalm 138:7

Today's psalm is a hymn of thanksgiving to God, calling us to ponder his goodness with grateful hearts. It asks me to recognize how God has saved and held me, how the words of God have given me comfort and strength.

So I take time to reflect on the good things I have been given, the love held out to me unconditionally, and I offer a deep and profound expression of thanks. For I know that when I stretch out my hand to God, he leads me in sometimes unexpected ways.

This psalm also calls us to stretch out our own right hand and serve one another in response for all God has done in our lives.

Sit quietly for a few minutes and stretch out your right hand to God. Listen to what God might ask of you today.

Readings: Esther C:12, 14–16, 23–25; Psalm 138; Matthew 7:7–12

Friday, *February 22*

The Chair of Saint Peter the Apostle

Steppingstones

*"And I tell you, you are Peter, and on this rock
I will build my church...."*
—Matthew 16:18

Peter the Rock! Jesus intended an image of strength and stability. Today I would like to stretch the image of Peter the immovable to Peter the steppingstone, leading us into the future church.

Like Peter, we sometimes walk on water, but often sink into doubt. We applaud change and growth, yet stubbornly hold onto the past. We seek to love, yet limit our forgiveness. And like Peter, we are a mystery to ourselves.

With God's grace, we pray for courage never to become a stumbling block but a steppingstone to the unconditional love of God.

I will name the steppingstones of growth and freedom that have led me to this day and call me into the faith of my tomorrows.

Readings: 1 Peter 5:1–4; Psalm 23; Matthew 16:13–19

Saturday, *February 23*

Who Belongs?

"Your Father in heaven...sends rain on the righteous
and on the unrighteous."
—Matthew 5:45

Savor the comfort of God's pledge "to be your God" (Deut 26:17). Bask in the glow of God's unconditional love for you. Then look around. God's "treasured people" (Deut 26:18) includes unnumbered billions besides you. In God's beloved family, everyone belongs. All have a place at the table.

Such a wide circle of belonging challenges our human standards. God does not withhold gifts even from those who do evil. In God's eyes, no one wears the label *enemy*. What would it be like for me to see with God's vision, to love with God's heart, to meet even my adversary as sister or brother?

Pray by name for those whom you disagree with or dislike.

Readings: Deuteronomy 26:16–19; Psalm 119; Matthew 5:43–48

Darker the Night, Brighter the Light

Look up! Remember this promise:
"Look toward heaven and count the stars,
if you are able...."
—Genesis 15:5

Shopping malls, airports, even nightlights and digital clocks hide the stars. Don't be afraid of the dark. See how power outages can reveal a darkness that revels in the real.

Friend, into deep sleep descending as the sun is setting, deeper still is the darkening of fears, of doubts, of threats, of terrors lurking, looming even in the day. Look! From smoke a flaming forth consumes the carcasses in the holocaust—covenanting done!

Chosen, when suddenly the dazzling Promise of the Torah and Prophets is standing with you, are you terrified by the *Shekinah* of this Holy One in glory? Take courage; hold this moment in your silenced heart. Listen to him. Wait! Remember, "...for darkness is as light to you" (Ps 139:12).

Repeat, repeat!
"Come," my heart says, "seek his face!"
Your face, LORD, do I seek.
Do not hide your face from me (Ps 27:8–9).

Readings: Genesis 15:5–12, 17–18; Psalm 27;
Philippians 3:17—4:1, *or* Philippians 3:20—4:1;
Luke 9:28b–36

Monday, *February 25*

Truth Telling

*"For the measure you give will be the
measure you get back."*
—Luke 6:38

The psalmists keep reminding us to ponder what God has done for us. It is a story of love poured out without measure, "pressed down...running over" (Luke 6:38), a love that we do not deserve and cannot earn. Mercy, steadfast love, *hesed*, is God's way with us.

Truth to tell, we often turn from this love, rebelling, not listening. Why try to hide from it? This Lent, let us speak the truth about ourselves to God, to whom belong mercy and forgiveness.

The secret of mercy is to act as God does: "Do not condemn, and you will not be condemned" (Luke 6:37). But first, let's honestly admit to ourselves and to God that we have a long way to go.

**When you look in the mirror today, say to yourself,
"God knows all that I am and all that I am not.
God loves me beyond measure."**

Readings: Daniel 9:4b–10; Psalm 79; Luke 6:36–38

Getting It Right

Seek justice...
defend the orphan,
plead for the widow.
—Isaiah 1:17

What makes us good? God's answer is clear. Sacrifice, prayer, and ritual each has a place but are abhorrent in God's sight without acts that foster right relationship in the community. God cares about orphans, widows, aliens, the oppressed. God sees red, as it were, when we ignore or mistreat them. By hearing and responding to the cries of these forgotten ones, we give glory to God. This is the sacrifice of praise that God desires.

This Lent, write or call your government representatives to support laws that benefit persons who are poor.

Readings: Isaiah 1:10, 16–20; Psalm 50; Matthew 23:1–12

Wednesday, *February 27*

Cup of Life

But Jesus answered, "...Are you able to
drink the cup that I am about to drink?"
They said to him, "We are able." He said to them,
"You will indeed drink my cup."
—Matthew 20:22–23

At our baptism, we were received into the family of God and became disciples of Jesus. And as we walk the journey of this life, we do, indeed, drink his cup. Sometimes we taste the sweetness of our faith in him; other times, the bitterness of the cross. This is the same cup that led Jesus to fullness of life.

There is a story told about John Paul I, whose extraordinarily brief pontificate lasted a mere month. Someone asked about the pectoral cross he was wearing, a cross with the figure of the crucified Christ. When asked why he had chosen the crucifix rather than a plain cross, he answered simply, "Because the cross without Christ is too heavy to carry."

Whether my cup overflows with joy or bitterness, I will remember who first drank from this chalice of life.

Readings: Jeremiah 18:18–20; Psalm 31; Matthew 20:17–28

Walking in Truth

*"There was a rich man...who feasted sumptuously
every day. And at his gate lay a poor man named
Lazarus...who longed to satisfy his hunger with
what fell from the rich man's table."*
—Luke 16:19–21

This is a parable Jesus tells about what is important in life.
The Pharisees thought wealth was a sign of God's blessing
and poverty of God's curse. Wealth and status are not
character flaws, but neither are they guarantees of our
standing with God.

Our attitudes and choices, not possessions, are what
make us precious in God's sight. To see the face of God in
the face of another is to accept the responsibility of being
a brother or sister in the Lord. So I am challenged today
to live not in comparison but in relationship.

**Jesus, guide the eyes of my soul. Do not let me seek
for guarantees, but to live in hope that you
will show me the path of life.**

Readings: Jeremiah 17:5–10; Psalm 1; Luke 16:19–31

Rejection or Jealousy?

"The stone that the builders rejected has become the cornerstone;...it is amazing in our eyes.'"
—Matthew 21:42, quoting Psalm 118

Joseph, son of Jacob, and Jesus have something significant in common: rejection by those who should have known better. Joseph showed consideration for his father's wishes and earned his brothers' envy. Jesus taught people their responsibilities to the Father. He won the approval of the crowds but hatred from the chief priests and scribes.

We, too, can find ourselves in surprising situations. Seeking to lead others by Jesus' teachings, we can be condemned or excluded by the very people who perhaps by profession or ministry know more than we do. An exaggerated sense of competition or jealousy can cloud the brightest of minds. Jesus tells us that it is the Lord's doing and we should rejoice.

O God, let us remember that all can speak your word of truth. Let us not fear to share our insights and to receive the insights of others.

Readings: Genesis 37:3–4, 12–13a, 17b–28a; Psalm 105; Matthew 21:33–43, 45–46

Remembering Steadfast Love

Bless the LORD*, O my soul,*
and do not forget all his benefits....
—Psalm 103:2

Not long ago a small earthquake reminded me of a larger one in which I had narrowly escaped being crushed. Musing on that experience, I wrapped myself once again in a profound sense of gratitude.

"If I had died that day," I thought, "I would not have met...nor gone to...nor worked in...."

The joys that have filled two decades of my life, great experiences and dear friends, crowded into my awareness. I listed them in a way I had never done before, blessing God for each one and feeling a sense of the care God had poured on me even in the sorrows and challenges of those years. My morning reverie stretched into a canticle of thanksgiving.

"God, if you take me home today, it's okay. I've had a ball!" I prayed.

Loving God, let me live aware of your goodness,
so that I may thank you for your blessings.

Readings: Micah 7:14–15, 18–20; Psalm 103;
Luke 15:1–3, 11–32

The Burning Bush

God called to him out of the bush, "Moses, Moses!"
—Exodus 3:4

What was it about the burning bush that attracted Moses and continues to attract us today? It was fully ablaze, yet not consumed by the fire. In turning from his everyday task to see this unusual sight, Moses heard the call of God.

God calls to us too, attracting our attention through burning bushes. He longs to set our hearts on fire with a love that fills us but does not consume us. He patiently waits for us to turn toward him.

Where are places of burning bushes for us? Where do we turn when we step aside from our everyday lives? Perhaps it is a favorite walking path, a particular view on the ride to work, or a meal with a soul friend.

I will take some time today to step aside and turn my entire attention to God, saying, "Here I am" (Exod 3:4).

Readings: Exodus 3:1–8a, 13–15; Psalm 103;
1 Corinthians 10:1–6, 10–12; Luke 13:1–9

Monday, *March 4*

Desiring

*Hope in God; for I shall again praise him,
my help and my God.*

—Psalm 42:5–6a

Thirst, desire, hope—these words imply a felt absence. The psalmist thirsts to be able to praise God again. Naaman desires health. Jesus hopes his neighbors will have faith in him.

I recognize the cry of the psalmist. How often his thirsting words have been repeated in me!

Less often have I echoed his trust that God is ever present through times of discouragement or challenge. Oh yes, my head knows that. Yet I forget. I sometimes trust more in my own efforts even as I pray for help.

Jesus does not walk away from me; he stays the course, and I come again to a moment of recognition and praise. May my faith and trust grow. May I know more deeply that just as he is guiding this universe, he is guiding my life!

My soul thirsts for you, O God. I put my trust in you.

Readings: 2 Kings 5:1–15b; Psalm 42; Luke 4:24–30

Learning

*Make me to know your ways, O LORD;
teach me your paths.*

—Psalm 25:4

Each Lent I hear the words *with a contrite heart* and try to dispose my heart accordingly. Today the readings remind me of when I have had reason to be contrite before God, when I have had to face the painful fact of my own sinfulness. What do I learn from such moments?

What do we as a nation learn when similarly confronted? Do we even recognize our own sinfulness? Azariah's prayer for help is based on his awareness of God's mercy; he relies only on God's fidelity to his covenant. He has learned the great lesson of life: "For you are just in all you have done" (Dan 3:27).

God, when I act from the least of who I am, I must learn that I can depend only on your steadfast love for me. Let me not be like the wicked steward (Matt 18) who learned nothing from the master's forgiveness. Teach me to be your compassion.

**Help me to be awake to the
opportunities to be compassionate!**

Readings: Daniel 3:25, 34–43; Psalm 25; Matthew 18:21–35

Letter and Spirit

*"Unless your righteousness exceeds that of
the scribes and Pharisees, you will never
enter the kingdom of heaven."*
—Matthew 5:20

The scribes and Pharisees put on a good face by observing the letter of the Law perfectly and demanding that others do so as well. Jesus called them hypocrites, whitened sepulchers. What they lacked was the spirit of the Law, which is love of God and love of neighbor, as exemplified in the Beatitudes.

As we move through these Lenten days, let us pray for and act out of the love that Jesus taught us through his words and example.

**Today, Lord, help me not to lay burdens of expectation
on others. Instead, may I help to lighten their
burdens by my love and support.**

Readings: Deuteronomy 4:1, 5–9; Psalm 147; Matthew 5:17–19

God: Transcendent, Immanent

O come; let us worship and bow down,
let us kneel before the LORD, our Maker!
For he is our God,
and we are the people of his pasture,
and the sheep of his hand.

—Psalm 95:6–7

Lent is a good time to ponder our relationship to God, who is both transcendent and immanent. We kneel before him in worship as the One who created all, is above all, and is over all; the One who is beyond our ability to grasp or understand. We can only kneel in awesome wonder before this transcendent God.

At the same time, God shares our lives intimately as a shepherd guiding and guarding us through the dangers of life. God's loving presence pervades all our thoughts, words, and actions. God is closer to us than we are to ourselves, present and creating in every cell of our being.

O great and awesome God, let me feel
your tender love in all the events of today!

Readings: Jeremiah 7:23–28; Psalm 95; Luke 11:14–23

Friday, *March 8*

No Greater Love

"Come back to me with all your heart;
don't let fear keep us apart."
—"Hosea," Gregory Norbet

Hosea's call invites us to turn from our sinful ways, not out of fear of God but out of love. He reminds us of how many times God's love prevailed over the hard-hearted Israelites.

The Gospel tells of the scribe trying to trick Jesus into misspeaking. To the question "Which commandment is the first of all?" (Mark 12:28), Jesus as always gives a straightforward answer. He says that total love of God—heart, soul, strength, and mind—is primary and that love of neighbor is like it. Like God's, this love is both giving and forgiving.

To truly love God we must also love our neighbors, giving to them out of the bounty we have received from God and forgiving them as we have been forgiven by God.

"All things work together for good for those who love God"
(Rom 8:28).

God, may today be such a time for me.

Readings: Hosea 14:2–10; Psalm 81; Mark 12:28–34

The Desire of the Heart

For I desire steadfast love....
—Hosea 6:6

Today's readings call me to examine my prayer life. Hosea invites me to be attentive and mindful so that I can meet God who wants my love and friendship. In the Gospel, the tax collector stands before God in truth and honesty. Has he, like Hosea, already encountered God's incredible love, a love that is unconditional and forgiving, so that he can stand in his truth knowing that he is loved?

Loving God, my actions and preoccupations say a lot about me. You know me as I am and as I desire to be. Give me your grace to see you as a loving God, and to be grateful for your love. I praise you for your faithfulness. Help me to be more aware of your presence in my life.

Today I will find a place of quiet to look into my prayer life.
When was I mindful of God's activity in my life?
For what was I grateful?

Readings: Hosea 6:1–6; Psalm 51; Luke 18:9–14

Who's Coming to Dinner?

"Still far off, his father saw him and...ran and put his arms around him and kissed him."
—Luke 15:20

"This son of yours...devoured your property....I have been working like a slave for you, and...never disobeyed."

"Son,...all that is mine is yours. But...this brother of yours...dead...has come to life." (Luke 15:30, 29, 31–32)

Please! Come in, eat, celebrate!

God was reconciling the world to himself, not counting their trespasses...and entrusting the message of reconciliation to us. (2 Cor 5:19)

How do I enable this new creation? Do I recognize in my words or behavior the grumbling Pharisee-in-me? Am I the good and faithful servant, full of dutiful obedience, frustrated by those who *get away with it*? Am I angered by *those people*? By those who have wronged me? At whose table will I sit?

Let me taste and see your goodness, Lord. Fill my heart with your compassion so that, with you, I too may be close to "the broken-hearted...the crushed in spirit" (Ps 34:18).

Readings: Joshua 5:9a, 10–12; Psalm 34; 2 Corinthians 5:17–21; Luke 15:1–3, 11–32

Faith Works Wonders

For I am about to create new heavens
and a new earth....
—Isaiah 65:17

The royal official who believed that Jesus could cure his son took the risk to invite Jesus to his home. Jesus responded to the desire of his heart, cured his child, and created a whole new world for that family.

I am the compassion of Jesus in this world. Those who come seeking my help often take a risk. Do I appreciate this reality? Could I be their last resort after other attempts to get help have failed? Am I welcoming?

Loving God, every day you work wonders through the work of faithful witnesses. Give me attentive ears and an open heart to hear the voice of the needy. Help me believe that the help I am able to provide will let them experience your reign on earth. May your kingdom come!

Today I will respond to a person in need and
help create a new reality for them.

Readings: Isaiah 65:17–21; Psalm 30; John 4:43–54

In a Place to Be Noticed

"Stand up, take your mat, and walk."
—John 5:8

Think of this crippled man who has been sick for thirty-eight years. He comes to the pool of Bethesda often, perhaps every day, hoping that someone will notice his plight and help him into the pool. He is ignored and passed by, but he is faithful to putting himself where he can be noticed. And one day, the Son of God comes by and takes notice. The place where he has experienced the rejection of many becomes the blessed place where he meets Jesus for the first time and knows care, concern, and cure. He expected the stirring waters of the pool to be the source of a cure but it is the person of Jesus who grants him his heart's desire.

Today let us notice the ignored or challenged people in our world. Let us open our hearts and be the face of Jesus for them.

Readings: Ezekiel 47:1–9, 12; Psalm 46; John 5:1–16

Wednesday, *March 13*

Recommitment

And I will turn all my mountains into a road....
—Isaiah 49:11

On Ash Wednesday, the church called each of us to recommit ourselves to Gospel living, and so we made our resolve to overcome some habit that keeps us from living the Gospel fully, or we decided to move out of our comfort zone to follow Christ more closely. Keeping our resolve has required mindfulness, prayer, and repeated efforts. Sometimes to keep on going is very difficult. Climbing mountains is hard work!

Yet as we continue responding to the Spirit in overcoming former habits, we find ourselves moving more consistently in a new direction. God is making of our mountains a new road.

Experienced mountain climbers never go alone: nor do we. This Lent, the whole church is moving over mountains that are becoming the way to resurrection and fullness of life.

Today I will recommit myself to my Lenten resolve.

Readings: Isaiah 49:8–15; Psalm 145; John 5:17–30

Gratitude

O give thanks to the LORD, for he is good;
for his steadfast love endures forever.

—Psalm 106:1

What an incredible mystery that the infinite God, who is absolute Love, is my constant companion throughout my life from birth to death! Dwelling in the deepest part of my being, God is an unwavering presence to whom I can turn at any time with utter confidence.

O faithful God, I can recall so many times in my life when I was aware of your presence, especially when I needed it most...when I had hard decisions to make...in the midst of a painful loss...in my times of failure, disappointment, and loneliness. In all the ups and downs of my daily life, your love upholds me. I am overwhelmed with gratitude and I thank you for your unchanging love.

Give thanks today for a few of the times you were aware of God's steadfast love.

Readings: Exodus 32:7–14; Psalm 106; John 5:31–47

My Way of Life

He became to us a reproof of our thoughts;
the very sight of him is a burden to us,
because his manner of life is unlike that of others....

—Wisdom 2:14–15

The Wisdom writer is speaking of the challenge good people pose to those who do evil. He speaks first of those who seek the good life, who oppress the poor, and who disregard the needy; then he considers the good person who opposes that way of thinking.

As I ponder the Wisdom words, I wonder if my conversations lead others to examine their own thoughts about the unjust systems in our society. Do I discuss political policies that affect the poor and disenfranchised with those who disagree with me, even if it causes me discomfort? More importantly, I wonder if the way I live speaks Gospel values to those I encounter. Do my decisions and actions offer alternatives of justice and compassion?

Today I will consider whether my actions match my words.

Readings: Wisdom 2:1a, 12–22; Psalm 34;
John 7:1–2, 10, 25–30

Becoming

"This is the Messiah."
—John 7:41

Fallout from a world-changing invitation: *Come to me for living water*.

The unpredictable arrival of Spirit—Sophia incarnate in Jesus stirs our hearts to receive LOVE. But what!…Such a stirring…Even the possibility of opening to LOVE within and without elicits fear, confusion, anger from the part of ourselves that clings to moral laws and doctrines to shield our controlling selves from deep thirst, from loneliness, need, anguish, pain—without and within.

> I would love to live
> like a river flows,
> carried by the surprise
> of its own unfolding.
> —John O'Donohue

Are you listening to your heart?

Jesus wants us to receive abundant life in communion with one another.

Step out of the confinement of the law, of expectations with no room for newness.

We are called to a becoming—a heart-to-heart relationship with Jesus and one another.

That's the invitation.

…Are you becoming?

Be touched by LOVE this day—
Surprise someone with your LOVE for them.

Readings: Jeremiah 11:18–20; Psalm 7; John 7:40–53

Fifth Sunday of Lent, *March 17*

Who Is Without Sin?

When they kept on questioning him, he straightened up and said to them, "Let anyone among you who is without sin be the first to throw a stone at her."
—John 8:7

I'm filled with discomfort because I identify so strongly with the scribes and Pharisees as they stand watching Jesus writing in the dirt. Each one fidgets, trying to appear disinterested, yet fearful that his secret sins will be exposed in the light of day. Their trick has backfired: Jesus avoids the trap of contradicting the Law, while treating the woman according to the Law he brings. Unable to cast a stone, each man slinks away in shame, leaving the woman free of condemnation, free to accept the grace of God in her life.

Seventeenth-century author François de La Rochefoucauld wrote, "Hypocrisy is the homage vice pays to virtue." God, make me more aware of the hypocrisy in my life. Grant me grace to turn from vice to virtue.

Readings: Isaiah 43:16–21; Psalm 126; Philippians 3:8–14; John 8:1–11

Wisdom's Ways

"Neither do I condemn you."
—John 8:11

Some are trying to trick Jesus into betraying his deepest identity as, what theologian James Alison calls, "Forgiveness in Person." Jesus changes the terms of the conversation for all. He silently bends down, writes with his finger on the ground, and then rises up. In my imagination, I see him tracing a spiral on the ground that turns to a rainbow in the sky as he enters into silent communion with Sophia and prays for each of us. Jesus would draw us into this communion so that we can LIVE DIFFERENTLY.

In his poem "Hagia Sophia," Thomas Merton writes of "a silence that is a fount of action and joy. It rises up in wordless gentleness and flows out to me from the unseen roots of all created being, welcoming tenderly, saluting me with indescribable humility."

Caught in false righteousness or looking for love in the wrong places?
Let us receive this wordless gentle FORGIVING LOVE AND LAMENT LOUDLY:
today there are places in our world where women are stoned
LIVE DIFFERENTLY.

Readings: Daniel 13:1–9, 15–17, 19–30, 33–62, *or* Daniel 13:41c–62; Psalm 23; John 8:1–11

Tuesday, *March 19*

Saint Joseph, Spouse of the Blessed Virgin Mary

Scandal and the Spirit

...steadfast love and faithfulness go before you.
—Psalm 89:14

Being a just man...Joseph faced a searing dilemma. According to the Law, if a young betrothed woman was found to have previously lost her virginity, she was to be stoned to death....Mercifully Joseph decided to divorce his wife quietly....

Just as the couple was on the verge of breaking up, an angel of the Lord appeared to Joseph in a dream, encouraging him not to be afraid to take his wife to his home for "the child within her is of the Holy Spirit."

In the midst of dangerous trouble, something holy is going forward. God's Spirit moves amidst the threatening situation. (Elizabeth Johnson, *Truly Our Sister*)

Does the image of Joseph, empowered by Spirit, going beyond the Law to protect Mary and the new life stirring in her startle you?

Have you felt called in compassion to go beyond the law? Did you?

Readings: 2 Samuel 7:4–5a, 12–14a, 16; Psalm 89; Romans 4:13, 16–18, 22; Matthew 1:16, 18–21, 24a, *or* Luke 2:41–51a

Wednesday, *March 20*

Turning Away from Idolatry

"If our God whom we serve is able to deliver us from
the furnace of blazing fire and out of your hand,
O king, let him deliver us. But if not, [know],
O king, that we will not serve your gods and we will
not worship the golden statue that you have set up."
—Daniel 3:17–18

The young men are citizens in good standing, serving as administrators in Babylon. But faithful to the covenant, they refuse to worship the idol, the king's creation. Their faith in the God of Abraham gives them the courage to defy the king, to cast aside their lives of comfort and privilege, and to face the blazing furnace. Without the certainty of divine intervention, they nonetheless choose fidelity and obedience to the God of their ancestors.

Increase my courage and my confidence in you,
O God, as I face the challenges of this day.

Readings: Daniel 3:14–20, 91–92, 95; Daniel 3:52–56; John 8:31–42

Our Prodigal God

*"I will establish my covenant between me and you,
and your offspring after you throughout their
generations, for an everlasting covenant, to be
God to you and to your offspring after you."*
—Genesis 17:7

Perhaps nothing more conveys God's eternal generosity than the covenant he makes with Abraham and his descendants. This covenant is not a legal contract binding two parties, but a one-sided grant, a guarantee made by the more-powerful party to another who has much less to bring to the bargaining table. God takes on the obligation to be the God of Abraham and his descendants until the end of time, binding the creator of the universe to his creatures. All God asks in return is fidelity and obedience, a request hardly on a par with what is bestowed on humans.

May I—an heir to that ancient covenant—live in awe of the boundless generosity of God in the history of salvation. Today may I respond to God's love with greater fidelity and obedience.

Readings: Genesis 17:3–9; Psalm 105; John 8:51–59

Living with Integrity

*"Even though you do not believe me, believe the
works, so that you may know and understand."*
—John 10:38

Jesus clearly did not just *do his own thing*. His actions were always in conformity to the will of his Father.

Do I live with such integrity that I invite others to know and understand me based on my behavior? Or am I prone to seek to be understood by explaining or justifying my actions, some of which may be at odds with what I profess to be most important to me?

Today, I will try to be a person of integrity, so that what I do and what I say are all of a piece. I will be mindful that my words and my actions need to reflect my deepest commitments and desires.

"O LORD of hosts, you test the righteous,
you see the heart and the mind" (Jer 20:12).

Incline my thoughts, my desires,
and my works toward your will this day, O God!

Readings: Jeremiah 20:10–13; Psalm 18; John 10:31–42

Gather the People

Then they shall be my people, and I will be their God.
—Ezekiel 37:23

At first glance, there is quite a contrast between the first and second readings. Ezekiel speaks glowingly of the time when the people will live in peace and unity on the land God has given them; indeed, God will dwell *with* them. The Gospel presents the rant of the Pharisees seeking to arrest Jesus. Speaking in his role as high priest, Caiaphas prophesies that Jesus will need to die for the people, both the Jewish people and all the "dispersed children of God" (John 11:52). Here, unity will be achieved, but at a great price.

We live in a world fragmented by misunderstandings, wars, inequalities. Families, nations, churches are wracked by disharmony. Only when we allow God, Shepherd and Lord, to gather us together will true peace and unity be achieved.

Today I will pray for a person with whom I am not in unity.

Readings: Ezekiel 37:21–28; Jeremiah 31:10–13; John 11:45–56

Palm Sunday of the Passion of the Lord,
March 24

Take a Stand

Those assembled accused Jesus of "perverting our nation...saying that he himself is the Messiah....[He] stirs up the people by teaching...."
—Luke 23:2, 5

We hear how Pilate dissembles: pandering to the crowd, surrendering to mob pressure, conjuring friendship from enmity—treachery with a smile. He three times affirms this man as not guilty. People stand by watching as soldiers mock and leaders scoff. Shouts of "Crucify, crucify him!" (Luke 23:21) prevail. Even as he hangs dying, people stand by, watching soldiers gamble and leaders taunt.

In the midday's darkening, the leading soldier-guard declares, "Certainly this man was innocent" (Luke 23:47).

"All his acquaintances...stood at a distance, watching" (Luke 23:49).

Where do I stand?

At such a spectacle am I an observer or a participant? Do I avoid this sort of thing? Or do I protest? Play it safe?

How do I stand? Up? Out? For? With? By? Aside? In?

Let the questions haunt me on this day of processions; where am I in the crowd?

Readings: Luke 19:28–40 (Entrance Procession); Isaiah 50:4–7; Psalm 22; Philippians 2:6–11; Luke 22:14—23:56, *or* Luke 23:1–49

Called, Grasped, Shaped

*I am the LORD, I have called you in righteousness,
I have taken you by the hand and kept you....*

—Isaiah 42:6

Do I believe that I have been called by God? Called to a way of living? Called to develop my gifts? Given chances to grow that are unique to me?

When times were tough, did I feel called, grasped, and shaped by a friend, a prayer, an event that spoke just to me?

And how has *God* shaped me to carry the unique responsibilities of my life? There is surely a story in that journey, my own inimitable salvation history.

Just as Jesus was called, grasped, and shaped by God, by his parents, by the people he met along his journeys, and by his reflective moments, I too develop and grow.

**Take some time to reflect on your unique circumstances,
gifts, and responsibilities. How has God shaped you
to be a light to others?**

Readings: Isaiah 42:1–7; Psalm 27; John 12:1–11

Tuesday of Holy Week, *March 26*

It's Time to Forgive

...and my God has become my strength....
—Isaiah 49:5

I've betrayed. I've been betrayed.

In either case there is deep hurt and a sense of loss. I dwell in my pain, and it's usually a while before I am able to take this pain to God.

Jesus is aware that the forces of evil are slowly, inexorably moving in on him; that his life is coming to an end. One of his own has set the final betrayal in motion. And a betrayal of another kind will also take place: Peter is not yet able to walk the walk of fidelity.

Where does Jesus receive the strength to forgive? He turns to Abba and puts his trust in the God who is always there for him.

Today I will ask for strength to forgive those who have betrayed me and to seek forgiveness of those whom I have betrayed.

Readings: Isaiah 49:1–6; Psalm 71; John 13:21–33, 36–38

Conspiring with Jesus

"Surely not I, Lord?"
—Matthew 26:22

Jesus foretells his betrayal, and the disciples, keenly aware of their own human weakness, ask with trepidation if they could be the one to betray their Lord. Only the opportunist Judas, who has already betrayed Jesus in his heart, asks the question insincerely.

Judas's conspiracy with the religious authorities to hand over Jesus led to today's traditional name, *Spy* Wednesday.

Jesus also conspires, not to betray, but to obey the unfolding will of God. He takes his place among us, reads the secrets of our hearts, and invites us into union with him, even to his way of suffering.

Today, Jesus, I will *conspire* with you to examine my attitudes and behaviors. Surely, yes, I am capable of thinking and acting in ways that betray my commitment to you. Today I will look for an opportunity to choose fidelity over betrayal in my following of you.

Readings: Isaiah 50:4–9a; Psalm 69; Matthew 26:14–25

Re-Membering

"Do this in remembrance of me."
—1 Corinthians 11:24

Remembering, recalling, and reliving prior experience may seem to be more a task of later years, when the memories of time past outweigh stamina and opportunity for outward action. But the intricately detailed formation of memory traces, their depth and range, is highly dependent on our level of attentiveness and investment of ourselves in the experience. Who and what we are most present to in the moment determines the very structural changes that occur in our brains. Not only our memories but our motivation and emotions are affected by the patterns thus formed.

On this Holy Thursday night, I will attend fully to the breaking of the bread, the sharing of the cup, and the washing of feet. I will seek to open each sense to the Passover experience in order to remember and be transformed by my participation.

Readings, Evening Mass of the Lord's Supper:
Exodus 12:1–8, 11–14; Psalm 116; 1 Corinthians 11:23–26; John 13:1–15

Good Friday, *March 29*

The Tomb of Jesus

The tomb was nearby, [and] they laid Jesus there.
—John 19:42

The Passion that we hear today is taken from the Gospel of John. It concludes with the burial of Jesus in "a new tomb in which no one had ever been laid" (John 19:41).

From the ancient days of the Egyptians to the present, there has prevailed a custom of placing special objects in the casket or tomb of a newly deceased person. What might *you* place in the tomb of Jesus? Is there a word, a place, a song, a memento?

Take some time today to visualize yourself visiting Jesus' tomb. Linger for a while and pray. Then place your special object there before you move on.

Readings, Celebration of the Lord's Passion:
Isaiah 52:13—53:12; Psalm 31; Hebrews 4:14–16, 5:7–9; John 18:1—19:42

Holy Saturday, *March 30*

Where Life Abides

"Why do you look for the living among the dead?"
—Luke 24:5

How often I spend time and energy pursuing plans, goals, relationships that have already withered and died!

I hold onto an old reality when something new is being offered. What I need is to become attuned to the deep desires of my heart.

It's always more, it's always better. God does not disappoint.

It's the resurrection story, and it's mine.

**Let me spend some time today discerning
where there is new life for me.**

Readings, Vigil Mass: Genesis 1:1—2:2; Genesis 22:1–8;
Exodus 14:15—15:1; Exodus 15:1–18; Isaiah 54:5–14;
Isaiah 55:1–11; Baruch 3:9–15, 32—4:4; Ezekiel 36:16–28;
Romans 6:3–11; Psalm 118; Luke 24:1–12

Believing Is Seeing

Therefore, let us celebrate the festival....
—1 Corinthians 5:8

John's Gospel has Mary Magdalene coming to the tomb alone. It is dark, a necessary element in his story, bespeaking the absence of the glaring lights and noise of daytime. Only moon and stars bear mute witness to her journey. In the sacred time just before dawn, she is able to center her heart on the hope she is feeling: the possibility of resurrection.

But it's too much even for her. The rolled-away stone seems proof of some nefarious deed on the part of unbelievers.

I've been there, Mary. I've refused to believe what my heart tells me is true, allowing preconceived ideas to overshadow reality. Like you, I've run away from the truth.

Jesus comes to us, calls us by name, gently urging us to see and believe.

**Today I want to be with Jesus in the garden of
the resurrection, where no proofs are needed, only love.**

Readings: Acts 10:34a, 37–43; Psalm 118;
1 Corinthians 5:6b–8, *or* Colossians 3:1–4; John 20:1–9

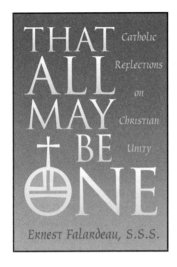

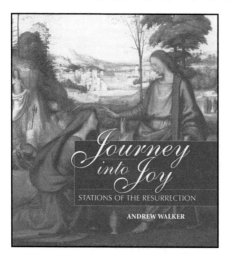

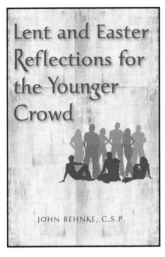

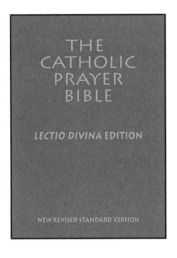

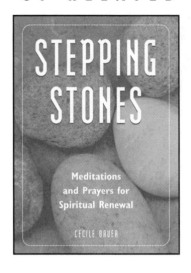

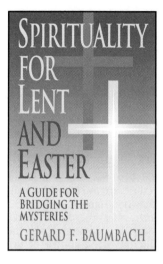

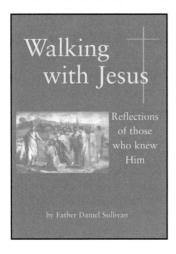

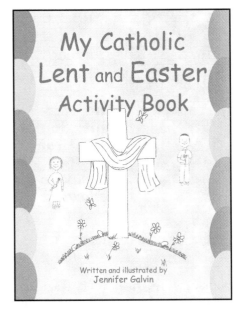

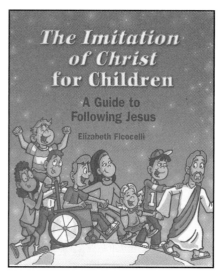

Living the
Days of Lent
2014

EDITED BY
Ellen Dauwer, SC AND
Mary McCormick, SC

Makes a Great Gift!

Living the Days of Lent 2014

Paulist's best-selling series of daily Lenten devotions uses scripture, prose reflections, and original prayers and poems to center readers' minds and souls and gently bring them to readiness for Easter. With these daily meditations, readers learn to open themselves to the risks and rewards of living a fuller life, of finding compassion from themselves and others, and of resting more deeply in God's loving care.

Living the Days of Lent 2014—
- runs daily from Ash Wednesday through Easter Sunday.
- ends each day's selection with the daily lectionary citations.
- includes pointed challenges for one's thoughts and actions.
- comes in a tear-out, page-a-day format for handy use.

-------------------------------- *Reserve Your Copy Today!* --------------------------------

Please send me _____ copy(ies) of: **Living the Days of Lent 2014**
978-0-8091-4777-9 @ **$4.95 ea.**

Please include applicable sales tax, and postage and handling ($3.50 for first $20 plus 50¢ for each additional $10 ordered)—check or money order only payable to **Paulist Press.**

Enclosed is my check or money order in the amount of $ _____

Name _____

Position _____

Institution _____

Street _____

City/State/Zip _____

Phone # _____

For more information or to receive a free catalog of our publications, contact us at:

Paulist Press™ 997 Macarthur Blvd., Mahwah, N.J. 07430 • 1-800-218-1903
FAX 1-800-836-3161 • E-MAIL: info@paulistpress.com • www.paulistpress.com
Prices subject to change without notice.